CHAPTER I: INTRODUCTION

This study concerns intelligence collection at the tactical level. Specifically, it reveals a lack of collection assets in the division of a contingency corps operating in an immature corps. Inherent to the division of a contingency corps is rapid strategic deployability of forces into hostile areas to demonstrate US resolve. However, this very imperative of contingency operations is an impediment to intelligence collection, the most critical mission for that division immediately upon arrival in theater.

Generally, a combat commander will be reluctant to use critically short deployment space on board his air force transports for anything other than weapon systems that kill enemy troops. His need for intelligence remains as critical as his need for rapid strategic deployability, yet these two requirements are normally mutually exclusive. What asset is available to meet this seemingly difficult task? The answer is his organic long-range surveillance detachment.

The good news is that the long range surveillance (LRS) teams are light weight, deployable, and a reliable means of accurate human intelligence (HUMINT) collection on enemy activity. The bad news is that there are not enough of them in the division of a contingency corps. There exists a gap between intelligence collection requirements and capabilities in the division of the contingency corps.

The limits of this study are self-imposed. I intend to conduct this examination with the clear knowledge that the emphasis for the army in the 1990's is crystallizing today: global contingency operations across the spectrum of conflict during a period of decreasing funds. The US Army must be able to do more with less. Intellectual honesty forces me to acknowledge the need to intensify research and development of technological advances in military hardware, but fiscal reality admonishes me not to be too enthusiastic about the fielding prospects of the future. Therefore, projected future systems will not be discussed, but the long-range surveillance assets at corps and division will.

In this study I will first establish the fundamental differences between a division and a corps by examining the theoretical foundation that distinguishes the two. Second, I will look at current doctrine covering both division and corps operations. These doctrinal writings will reveal that the echelon of command for the forward deployed corps is the same as the division of the contingency corps. Next, the study will investigate the intelligence collection gap in the force structure of the division of the contingency corps. Although the echelon of command is the same, the division in a contingency corps has fewer intelligence collection tools than forward deployed corps to perform similar missions. This creates a collection gap between mission requirements and resources provided by force design to accomplish those missions. Following that, I will examine LRS units as the possible means to close the collection gap. I will look at historical LRS antecedents as well as current LRS doctrine. In the next chapter, I will examine Soviet experience with LRS type units. The US army can learn how Soviet doctrine was shaped by combat and how Soviets use LRS type units today.

Before I assume my charted course, I must define several terms that are critical to the study: mature and immature theaters of operations, forward deployed and contingency corps, and reconnaissance and surveillance. A mature theater of operations has distinct unit boundaries, existing lines of communication and logistical facilities, a clearly understood command and control structure that may include allied or friendly foreign forces, and familiarity with the terrain. In general, a mature theater has forces that have been in place. The Federal Republic of Germany and the Republic of Korea are existing mature theaters.

In contrast, an immature theater enjoys none of these characteristics. Very little is predetermined; unit boundaries are indistinct and must be shaped; the command and control structure may be unclear; and forces may not have been invited in. Over time, possibly days or weeks, the theater will mature as more forces, combat, combat support, and combat service support, augment the forces in place. Immature theaters are far more common.[1]

Forward deployed forces are the result of our national security strategy of containment. They perform the function of demonstrating permanent US resolve in areas immediately contested by nations and ideologies inimical to US interests. Examples of forward deployed corps are V and VII US Corps in Germany and the Combined Field Army in Korea, a combined US-ROK force equivalent of a US corps.

The Army also has contingency forces that are prepared to bolster those forward deployed units in mature theaters or to meet challenges elsewhere in immature theaters. Although usually associated with force projection into immature theaters against a threat on the low intensity end of the conflict spectrum, contingency forces may face, for example, conventional Soviet forces in either Europe (mature) or Southwest Asia (immature). Regardless of threat or theater, rapid deployment is the signal characteristic of contingency forces. Examples of contingency corps are I Corps and XVIII Airborne Corps. III Corps is a contingency corps designated to reinforce NATO.

The final terms that require definition are reconnaissance and surveillance. The intended use of these two terms is quite distinct, but their respective meanings have become blurred. They are often used interchangeably; they clearly are not. Field Manual (FM) 101-5-1, Operational Terms and Symbols, defines reconnaissance as:

> a mission undertaken to obtain information by visual observation, or other detection methods, about the activities and resources of an enemy or potential enemy[2]

Reconnaissance is a directed effort whose purpose is specific to a particular place and time. Reconnaissance is the active means of gathering intelligence about the enemy to support particular friendly tactical or operational requirements. It may require fighting to obtain the desired information.

By comparison, surveillance, according to FM 101-5-1, is "a systemic observation of airspace or surface areas."[3] Surveillance does not have a specific intent or focus on the enemy. It seeks to determine by observation patterns or changes in the enemy's actions over extended periods. For example, surveillance may seek to establish trends in the deployment of enemy forces, his use of terrain, his levels of security. The sum of all of these observations may reveal a potential enemy weakness or intent that may be exploited.

Whereas reconnaissance is an active measure, surveillance is more passive.

CHAPTER II: THE FOUNDATIONS OF DIVISION AND CORPS

This chapter will look at the fundamental differences and similarities between the division in a contingency corps and a forward deployed corps. I will discuss briefly the development of the corps out of the division "cordon system" during the time of Napoleon. Next, I will compare and contrast the doctrinal differences and similarities between the division in a contingency corps and a forward deployed corps as explained in Field Manual (FM) 71-100, Division Operations, and FM 100-15, Corps Operations.

It is safe to say that Napoleon weaved the first threads from miltary classical strategy into the tapestry of operational art with the expansion of his division "cordon system" into corps. He alone mastered this early form of operational warfare until his defeat at Waterloo. Napoleon truly understood the marked advantage of combining divisions into larger groupings of corps. On the surface, this advantage was size, more infantry, more cavalry, and more artillery. More significantly, however, was the tactical flexibility of command and control that this increased size provided. It was the beginning of operational art.

Napoleon inherited a military system shaped by others. Specifically, the organizational moorings of

Napoleon's army trace to a German, Marshal Saxe. Inspired by Scipio, the great Roman consul, and his legions, Saxe fathered the earliest form of the division. Saxe's geometric proposal, four regiments in each division and four centuries in each regiment with some light infantry and cavalry, provided tactical flexibility and ease of maneuver in battle.[4]

The division was capable, therefore, of acting independently yet in concert with the army plan. This became the "cordon system." It demonstrated not only the linkage between strategy and tactics, but the primacy of the former. Strategy shaped tactics. The "cordon" fought (tactics) independently, yet was guided by a master plan (strategy). It had to be mobile, capable of exploiting the opportunities that good fortune or the enemy provided.

Yet Napoleon saw the inherent limitations of the "cordon." It had to fight as a mass; separated forces in independent engagements could result in the piecemeal destruction of the whole. Additionally, it was tied to a fixed system of supplies. Although a flexible organization, it retained flexibility only at the tactical level. Another level of warfare was required to bridge the chasm between strategy and its execution. A larger, self-sufficient army was needed.

Napoleon took Saxe's divisional organization from a unitary fighting force and expanded it into the

"Grande Armee," a force consisting of several corps and varying at times from 250,00 to over 400,000 soldiers. An army of this magnitude provided the freedom to seek battle and generally to ensure that it was on favorable terms. The corps was born and with it, in Jominian terms, "grand tactics,"[5] the embryonic form of operational art.

> Previously, the
>
> cordon system ... ultimately broke down into a
> series of uncoordinated division actions because
> no proper command, control, and communications
> systems existed to support such widely distributed
> forces.[6]

However, the corps formation expanded and deepened the battlefield without any loss in command and control of the larger units. This was "grand tactics." Operations conducted successively on separate pieces of terrain throughout the battlefield by these larger corps gave depth to what had previously been shallow and linear battle.[7] Operations in one location could influence the outcome of operations elsewhere.

Napoleon's campaign against the Prussians near Jena in 1806 is a desriptive example of the synergy of successive battles. As the French forces moved on a broad front along several routes near the River Saale in Saxony, Napoleon was able to commit his corps independently and quickly as they met Prussian resistance in the vicinity of Jena. Napoleon quickly

seized the initiative at Jena and overwhelmed his
adversary. At a distance of approximately 10 miles to
the north, one of his corps defeated a much larger
Prussian force in Auerstadt in what appeared to be an
independent action. However, these actions were linked
in time and space.

Marshal Davout, the French corps commander in
Auerstadt, was sent north to cut off the anticipated
Prussian retreat from Jena along the Prussian lines of
communication. Davout was unaware that the Prussians
had already begun their retreat to the north before
French forces under Napoleon's direct command attacked
in Jena. Running into the larger Prussian force in
Auerstadt, Davout defeated the piecemeal attacks by the
Prussians while Napoleon, in Jena, destroyed the
remaining Prussian forces left behind to cover their
retreat to the north. Although Prussian leadership was
suspect, the French achieved victory by a serendipitous
application of suc essive operations.[e]

The significant lesson learned from history is
that corps and divisions evolved for different
purposes. The division is a tactical organization; a
corps is a transitional command that links tactics to
something short of strategy -- the operational level of
war. The corps must be prepared to fight at the
tactical level but disposed to fight at the

operational. Corps is primarily "the link between operational and tactical levels of war."[9]

From these beginnings, the corps has evolved today into the forward deployed corps and the contingency corps. A forward deployed corps is defensive in nature. It still retains an offensive capability, but its primary mission is the defense, to await "the appearance of the enemy in front of our lines and within range."[10] General Crosbie Saint, US Army Commander in Europe as well as the Central Army Group Commander of NATO's Allied Forces Central Europe, established his command priority to be the execution of the "general defense plans"[11] for Central Army Group. In fact, the mission statements for his two US corps echo his defensive perspective. The mission of VII Corps is to "defend in sector"[12] while V Corps sees its mission to "defend in sector ... conduct counterattacks to restore the IGB (Inter-German Border)."[13]

It is apparent that the defensive posture of a forward deployed corps is not "an absolute defense"[14] characterized by passivity. Although the defense is a "shield made up of well directed blows,"[15] its purpose is preservation not conquest.

On the other hand, the contingency corps mission is conquest, to wrest something from someone. The act of projecting forces into a contested area is an offensive action. Like the forward deployed corps, the contingency corps is comprised of elements from both forms of warfare, offense and defense. The offense is the "constant alternation and combination of attack and defense."[16] The mission of the XVIII Airborne Corps at Fort Bragg is to "deploy forces into [country X] and conduct delay operations."[17] The offense, in this misson statement, is followed by a form of the defense, the delay. Accordingly, the 82nd Airborne Division, a division subordinate to XVIII Airborne Corps,

> conducts parachute/air land assault operations
> into [country X] to secure key facilities ...
> and to conduct defend/delay operations as forward
> as possible in zone.[18]

The contingency corps is an offensive corps, designed to conduct forced entry operations and to deny something to the enemy or to take something back from him.

Although the forward deployed corps and contingency corps have dissimilar missions, their force structures, specifically intelligence collection assets, are the same. The contingency corps needs intelligence pushed down to it before execution of any forced entry contingency mission. Its organic collection assets would mostly be ineffective and turned off until arrival in theater which often occurs after the shooting starts. By comparison, the forward deployed corps would have the same access to intelligence pushed down from army or national level as the contingency corps in addition to intelligence collected by its organic intelligence collection systems that are already in place, active, and hopefully reporting before hostilities.

Surprisingly, Army force structure provides similar intelligence collection assets to both types of corps but distinguishes between their respective warfighting requirements in army doctrine. FM 71-100, Division Operations, shows the different levels of modern warfare as strategic, operational, and tactical (see Diagram No. 1). This diagram depicts the echelons of command that are expected to fight at each level. This portrayal really does two things for Army doctrine. First, it groups Army forces as forward deployed and contingency. Second, the division commander of a contingency corps and the forward deployed corps commander are required to exercise the same echelon of command. The former is no surprise. The latter contradicts the theoretical foundation that distinguishes the echelons of command.

The doctrine is not consistent. A division, by design, is not a corps, yet army doctrine says it is. FM 71-100 tells the division in a contingency corps to perform at the same echelon of command as a forward deployed corps. However, the division is a tactical organization.

Divisions conduct close operations by fighting
their brigades and battalions ... It is the
outcome of the division close operations which will
ultimately determine the success or failure of the
division battle ... Successful division level
operations require the division to weight and
primarily concern itself with the division's close
operations.[19]

Close operations are the domain of the tactical

commander. Moreover, the division commander "must

develop superior tactics over the enemy to win."[20] The

division is a tactical echelon of command; the corps is

the link to the operational.

The critical link to the operational level of war

for a corps is its ability to see and to fight the

enemy throughout the depth of his formation. FM 100-15,

Corps Operations, further explains this fundamental

difference between division and corps level operations.

Whereas the division has to fight close, the corps must

"create and maintain the conditions for the success of

current battles and set up the conditions for the

success of future battles."[21] The corps helps the

division fight the current close battle while

simultaneously focusing the remainder of its attention

on the future close battle by conducting deep

operations now. In this role, the corps is the focal

point of AirLand Battle doctrine, synchronizing all

assets "to achieve tactical [division] and operational

[corps and higher] advantage over the enemy."[22] Simply

stated, the corps fights deep (see Diagram No.2).

This diagram addresses the corps battlefield structure. It indicates what corps must be able to do and how it needs to do it. First, what the corps must be able to do is synchronize in time and space its deep efforts with its close efforts. These two fights are not independent actions. It has to "decide what conditions can be created and exploited to defeat the enemy"[23] in the close fight. Second, how the corps goes about doing that is by shaping the battlefield. Shaping is the use of available resources to get the enemy to do something the friendly commander wants him to do, to set the terms for future engagements.

> Deep operations begin before the enemy closes with the corps and continue throughout the entire battle. The corps organic and supporting surveillance assets are initially used to locate and track ... the attacking enemy within the corps area of interest ... to identify and to strike selected high payoff targets to disrupt his ... dispositions, movements, and intentions.[24]

The ability to shape the battlefield further distinguishes corps from division.

In the final analysis, there are fundamental differences between a division and a corps. FM 100-5, Operations, states that "different levels of command perform different tactical and operational functions."[25] This statement seems clear enough. However, it does not apply when comparing the functions of a division in a contingency corps to those of a forward deployed corps.

The division in a contingency corps and a forward
deployed corps have to see deep and fight deep, the
ability to shape the battlefield. However, shaping the
battlefield involves more than the indiscriminate
pounding of the enemy as far back in his formation as
friendly weapons can reach. Shaping the battlefield, in
a theoretical sense, is a method to reduce uncertainty
and illuminate the enemy and his intentions. Shaping
will generally involve hitting the enemy but will
always involve seeing the enemy. Collection must
precede targeting.

Clausewitz characterized war as "the realm of
uncertainty," arguing that "three quarters of the
factors on which action in war is based are wrapped in
a fog of greater or lesser uncertainty."[26] The
commander at any echelon seeks to reduce uncertainty.
This involves seeing the battlefield. Clausewitz
experienced that in his day of cavalry which provided
speed and fluidity to battle "the commander continually
[found] that things [were] not as he expected."[27] If
that was an expected condition then, it is even more
pronounced today. The commander must expect the
unexpected and seek to make it certain. This entails
seeing and monitoring deep. Even the military genius
with the "appropriate gifts of intellect and
temperament ... to scent out the truth"[28] cannot devine
the dispositions of the enemy much less his intentions

15

without being able to know what he is up to beyond what can be seen from the front lines. Intelligence collection is how the commander can know the enemy.

An array of assets are available at both corps and division which complement each other and when deployed in depth can help the corps commander shape the battlefield. The division commander in a contingency corps is required to see deep like a corps but he does not have the same intelligence collection tools for the assigned task. This doctrinal contradiction remains unresolved and is the primary cause of the collection gap between requirements and capabilities.

CHAPTER III: THE COLLECTION GAP

I will briely review the force design for the intelligence collection assets and organizations at division and corps. The emphasis will be on LRS assets and a possible change in the force structure to address the deficiency in these assets at division.

The intelligence organizations at division and corps are the "functional equivalent of the old cavalry,"[29] whose historical role, in modern military parlance, was intelligence collection. The organic intelligence and electronic warfare organization at corps is the military intelligence (MI) brigade. In addition to other corps combat and combat support units whose missions include active intelligence collection such as the armored cavalry regiment and the aviation

16

brigade, the MI brigade is functionally organized to collect in all intelligence disciplines, to process, and to disseminate intelligence to the appropriate users in a timely manner. Assets at corps (see Diagram No.3) are designed to help the commander see deep. The assets that can provide the greatest depth are the fixed wing platforms and the long range surveillance company.

By contrast, the division intelligence collection assets in the organic MI battalion are similar to the assets available at corps but acquire at a shallower depth (see Diagram No.4). The division does not have the aerial exploitation assets available at corps. It does have a LRS detachment which is only a third the size of the company at corps. A more detailed explanation of LRS doctrine and organization will follow in the next chapter.

As with all other combat multipliers, intelligence collection assets are allocated down from echelon to echelon. Noticeably absent from the allocated support from corps to division are LRS assets (see Diagram No.5). Corps husbands aerial collection platforms and LRS teams for its own use. They are not task organized down to division.

It makes sense that corps retains its aerial exploitation assets for two reasons. First, the aerial assets have certain combat service support requirements

17

(instrumented airfield, certain communications links, electronic maintenance support) that division cannot provide without excessive augmentation from corps. Second, the aerial exploitation assets are only one of two "eyes" that the corps commander has to see deep in his area of influence. He would be ill-advised to give up such a scarce commodity. The other "eye" is the LRS company.

There is no operationally sound argument to husband LRS assets at corps especially in a contingency corps. LRS teams require no type of support not already in place for its organic LRS detachment. In a likely contingency corps scenario the division may be the highest echelon of command in theater for the duration of hostilities. The corps commander may intend to fight the war without deploying from home station, connected to his division commander on the ground via satellite communications, existing telephone lines, or facsimile machines. It makes no sense for a corps force structure to retain a collection asset that is light weight, quickly deployable in virtually any type of troop transport aircraft, transparent to the supported division's combat service support structure, and capable of seeing beyond the close battle.

This doctrinal inconsistency in the force structure for intelligence collection and the allocation of collection assets highlights the problem faced by the division commander of the contingency corps. He is expected to see deep like a forward deployed corps but does not have the collection capability to do it. The attendant collection gap must be closed. A force structure change can do it.

There is little doubt that the Army feels that LRS assets can help the division and corps commanders to "locate and attack enemy forces at extended ranges"[30] to a very high resolution for targeting. The army's need for tactical human intelligence collection was partially met in 1986 with the activation of a LRS detachment at division and a LRS company at corps. The need still exists in the division of the contingency corps. More LRS assets are needed at division, and corps has them.

CHAPTER IV: LONG RANGE SURVEILLANCE UNITS AS THE
COLLECTION GAP CLOSER

Even in this day of technological wonders, the individual soldier can have an immediate impact in an intelligence collection role. Tactical human intelligence in the form of LRS assets can meet the needs of commanders who have a look-deep mission. They are reliable and responsive to the commander.

> Even in this era of high technology,
> traditional patrols near or across enemy lines
> are still considered among the most reliable of
> human intelligence sources. Denied areas (those
> secured by the enemy) can be infiltrated by
> helicopter, parachute, sea, or on foot. Once in an
> advantageous and concealed position within a denied
> area, HUMINT team members make sketches, take
> notes, and photograph what they see.[31]

19

For a variety of reasons, corps and division commanders
want LRS assets available to them. All things
considered, a soldier on the ground observing but
unobserved by the enemy can measure the enemy force
like no technical sensors can. A sensor may provide
objective reporting but is incapable of a subjective
evaluation on an enemy that may be preparing to attack,
withdraw, or change its direction of movement -- all
critical and often ephemeral information about the
enemy that may impact on immediate friendly planning
and subsequent execution. A soldier, however, can gauge
a unit's morale, discipline, maintenance level, or
readiness.

History is rich with examples of intelligence
collection by soldiers on the ground and has proven
"that the best source of information is a soldier on a
radio saying,'this is what I see right now.'"[38] I
propose to look briefly at the historical antecedents
for the current LRS organizations at corps and
division.

The LRS units modern historical and organizational
predecessor was the scout, an element of the horse
cavalry that provided speed and information on the
enemy generally acquired from behind or within the
enemy's dispositions and always by direct observation.
Scouts were characterized by British General David
Henderson in his treatise, The Art of Reconnaissance,

as men of "natural aptitude ... [of] reason and
calculation"[33] and in short supply. Men of such
qualities were rare, but when these attributes surfaced
in the same individuals, "such men make history."[34]
Their objective, however, was not self-aggrandizement,
but rather the quiet task of gathering information on
the enemy, the "dry narrative of ascertained facts."[35]
Similar qualities no doubt are essential for today's
LRS team members and are as rare.

In World War II, a unique tactical organization
was created in the Pacific Theater of Operations, the
Sixth US Army Special Reconnaissance Unit, "The Alamo
Scouts."[36] Lieutenant General Walter Krueger, the Sixth
Army commander, learned many hard lessons about
amphibious operations and the need for a clear picture
of enemy dispositions in advance of landings. The
characteristically thick jungle canopy "frequently
reduced the usefulness of aerial reconnaissance"[37] as
the Japanese used the concealment to the advantage of
their operational preparations.

The Alamo Scouts were formed as a reconnaissance
unit to gather intelligence on the enemy dispostions
that could not be determined by other means. The scouts
were organized from the ranks of the Sixth Army. Their
mission "ranged from static surveillance to limited
direct action missions"[38] in advance of Sixth Army
operations. They enjoyed success during the invasion of

the Admiralty Islands in February 1944 and later the same year the landings at Leyte and on Luzon in the Philippines. In all cases they were able to infiltrate by seaborne landings behind enemy beach positions and report on enemy force locations, composition, and obstacles in time for the main body to adjust its invasion plan and further prepare for the beach assault.

In Vietnam, the long range reconnaissance patrols (LRRP) were used to gather intelligence on the enemy but had the associated mission to "disrupt operations, commit sabotage, and generally throw sand into the gears of the enemy war machine."[39] Because of the dual and often contradictory nature of its missions to gather information and to conduct direct action against the enemy, the doctrine for LRRP employment had no moorings; it was adrift. However, their success were well documented. In 1969, all LRRP companies were redesignated as Airborne Ranger Long Range Patrol Companies of the 75th Infantry Regiment. Each company was assigned to a division or field force (corps) headquarters. Long range ground reconnaissance had a role despite the vicissitudinary doctrine. It was to interdict the enemy where appropriate and report where the enemy was and where "his influences [did] not exist."[40] The army dropped LRRP's from the active component in 1974. They were replaced by "smart" sensors. Tactical HUMINT died.

The 1970's witnessed a military convalescence. The country and the military were recovering from the physical and emotional bleeding in Southeast Asia. Simultaneously, tactical human intelligence collection tied to the failure of the war lost favor. Technology infused the blood of those apparently weakened by the experience in Vietnam.

The loss of this valuable asset was transitory. Tactical HUMINT collection is now in the form of LRS units at corps and division. A large part of this resurgence is the "spread of insurgency and counterinsurgency warfare, or wars of national liberation"[41] that are not easily detected, observed, and certainly not analyzed by means other than human. The enemy is often the one who "dictates the limits and dimensions of the battlefield."[42] Low Intensity Conflict certainly is no exception. LRS assets can turn this around and allow the friendly commander to shape the battlefield in time and space according to his tactical and operational needs in light of the threat or its intentions.

The LRS company at corps consists of 18, 6 man teams. The division has a detachment comprised of four teams in a light division and six teams in all other types of divisions. Doctrinally, the LRS company can operate out to the limits of the corps commander's area of influence which is generally 150 kilometers forward of the front line of troops (FLOT). For planning purposes it can operate without replenishment for eight days. By comparison, the LRS detachment at division can operate out to 50 kilometers forward of the FLOT and can operate six days without resupply.

Diagram No.6 depicts a typical deployment pattern for corps and division LRS assets along a linear FLOT in a well defined corps area of operations. Corps detects deep while division tracks the enemy as he moves into the main battle area. The basic assumption upon which this doctrinal assertion is made is faulty for several reasons when considering contingency operations in an immature theater. Corps will likely not be in theater; the battlefield will probably not be linear; redundancy, an imperative of intelligence collection, is highly unlikely simply with the employment of divisional assets. These three points bear further explanation.

First, the corps commander will not necessarily be present in theater. The designation of corps boundaries is unlikely. The size and intentions of the threat may not require the physical presence of corps command and control headquarters and the associated combat support and combat service support elements. The anticipated or actual short duration of the fight may not warrant the buildup of higher command and control or logistic structure. The initial situation development in theater will be done by the division commander.

Second, the battlefield in a contingency operation may be as non-linear as it is linear. The non-linear battlefield is a more likely phenomenon and undoubtedly a confusing place. It is misleading to depict only a linear battlefield in doctrinal literature when a non-linear battlefield is just as likely.

Finally, integration of collected information from various sources is a form of verification and results in intelligence. Veification can also be accomplished by redundancy. Redundancy with LRS assets at division is nearly impossible to achieve because there are so few teams, and the battlefield is likely to expand in all directions. Although redundancy with LRS assets is not essential because of the reliability of a well trained human observer, the risks inherent in this type of tactical HUMINT operation warrants the use of teams in depth to ensure continuity of surveillance.[43]

Given the nature of contingency operations as described, it appears that LRS assets can ameliorate the problem of intelligence collection faced by the division commander inserted into an immature theater. LRS units are deployable by various means of infiltration (parachute, air land, helicopter, waterborne) and are a reliable method of helping the commander see deep beyond the immediate battle. The synergy of its light weight, deployability, and reliability categorizes LRS units ironically in the parlance of technology as a "genius" weapon. It is a system that has internal guidance, can be reprogrammed, is responsive, and can discriminate among the target array and pick out the one it needs to do something about whether that is to kill it, wound it, or, as is the case with LRS assets, simply report it.

The potential for LRS units as a system to close the collection gap has been discussed, but another issue concerning its applicability for the task must be addressed. A division commander in a contingency corps needs more LRS teams, but the force structure of today's army is a "zero-sum" proposition. The ultimate criteria for proposed force structure changes are how they affect readinesss and cost. Readiness must not decrease; costs cannot increase. The collection needs of the division commander in a contingency operation in an immature theater can be met rather easily, but not without challenges to the Army force structure.

The problem has been discussed. A division commander in a contingency corps is expected to perform the corps level mission to see deep. The division has insufficient intelligence collection assets to do it. He cannot increase his light weight at the cost of rapid deployability. When he projects his initial forces in theater, he must stabilize the close battle while developing the deep situation. He can not expect corps support for up to 96 hours, possibly more.

Current thought on deep operations is contained in the classified manual "Corps Deep Operations" dated September 1989. The unclassified sections of this manual describe deep operations as four days of synchronization, 96 hours in which to decide high payoff targets, detect those targets, and deliver ordnance on those targets. This three step process is called the D3 methodology of deep operations. The manual goes on to describe the "system of systems," sensors, processors, attack means, command and control, and communications, that holistically comprise the elements of deep operations (see Diagrams No.7 and 8).

The division commander in a contingency operation will only be able to establish his area of influence (the target area) upon arrival in theater, and this is usually after hostilities have started or are imminent. His only available means of detection will be his LRS detachment. Deep attack means are not his but will either self-deploy to the theater (airforce fighter-bombers) or will be enroute on subsequent air lift (attack helicopters or Multiple Launched Rocket System). His intelligence processors for target verification and classification will either be enroute to the theater if airlift is available or will remain

at home station to relay their data by long distance,
improved high frequency or satellite communications
paths if they are available. Corps command and control
in the form of the corps headquarters may be enroute as
well, depending on the situation.

There are many places in this synchronized, joint,
and sometimes combined effort where something may go
wrong. Things cannot go wrong with the detection phase.
Target acquisition is the Achilles heel of deep
operations. The commander cannot deliver on targets
that he cannot detect. The division commander with the
rapid deployment mission must enhance his detection
capabilities once in theater without increasing his
deployment criteria. LRS units were put back into the
Army force structure at corps and division to do that.
However, more is better. More LRS assets at division,
the echelon of command that by doctrine is expected to
employ them first and probably exclusively, and less at
corps is better.

The contingency corps does not need 18 teams. The
division in a contingency corps can use more than its
four or six teams. Corps does need an organic LRS
capability but not as much as it presently has. A
contingency requirement that templates an enemy threat
with intentions beyond 96 hours will probably involve
corps command and control in theater with the
associated intelligence collection assets form the MI

brigade. This includes LRS teams.

In this case, the corps commander will take battle handover from the division commander in place and may need to develop areas that the division commander could not cover with his assets. The corps commander can immediately, upon arrival in theater, insert his LRS teams without having to move in-place teams, a task he should avoid. Movement usually means compromise for the team.

The simple solution is to reapportion LRS assets from the contingency corps to its divisions. The following reapportionment is recommended. A contingency corps with two divisions should give up six teams for each division. The corps should retain the remaining six teams. In contingency operations, the division's gain must be the corps' loss.

This flies in the face of Army doctrine which teaches units to husband assets, to centralize the command and control of assets, and to enhance their efficiency. In fact, General Donn Starry, former commander of the Training and Doctrine Command, presaged the arrival of AirLand Battle in an important article in Military Review in March 1981 by stating that "the range of assets figuring in the battle is extended toward more emphasis on higher Army and sister service acquisition means and attack resources."[44] The interdependence among the services as stated by General

Starry to see and to fight deep is no less characteristic of the relationship between higher and lower echelons of command. However, efficiency with centralized command and control often detracts from effectiveness. This example is no exception.

Army doctrine teaches that a commander at any echelon of command must seek help from higher if he is faced with a situation that is about to exceed his abilities to cope. Formal restructuring in the form of permanent force design changes of assets from higher echelons of command to lower is not unprecedented, but institutional inertia as well as the prerogatives of command make it unlikely.

By contrast, the Soviet's doctrinal philosophy on force design is the exact opposite. They do not husband their assets at higher echelons of command. The Soviet use of norms or "performance standards"[45] creates a force structure with the requisite combat, combat support, and combat service support tools for a commander to accomplish given tasks. If he has to ask for more, he can probably expect a negative reply along with a request to name his successor.

CHAPTER V: SOVIET EXPERIENCE WITH LRS OPERATIONS

Soviet military experience demonstrates their heavy reliance on the human aspect of intelligence gathering or "razvedka." Like their US counterparts,

the Soviets have created an "ubiquitous and
comprehensive intelligence-gathering network"[46] and
will try to gather and process "quality of intelligence
rather than quantity of information."[47] These efforts
necessarily involve the use of sophisticated systems,
but "they will remain convinced that efficient
lower-level and human razvedka remains the key
ingredient of achieving success in battle."[48] I will
briefly discuss the Soviets "lower-level" and human
razvedka force structure and doctrine as it exists
today. I will follow with an historical look at the
Soviet use of LRS type units and lessons that can be
drawn from their experience specifically in the Kursk
and Vistula-Oder operations of World War II.

At the division level the Soviets place great
emphasis on human razvedka to help develop the tactical
situation. Every division has a reconnaissance
battalion comprised of two reconnaissance companies, a
radio and radar reconnaissance company, and a
reconnaissance assault company (RAC) which is
equivalent to the US LRS company found at corps. The
two reconnaissance companies perform close
reconnaissance from 30 to 50 kilometers forward of the
FLOT. The radio and radar assets are similar in
function but fewer in number to those found in the
military intelligence battalion in a US division. The
RAC, also referred to as the airborne reconnaissance

31

company or the long range reconnaissance company, "provides the division commander with a deep-look capability."[49]

Doctrinally, the Soviet RAC within the division will concentrate along "important axes, especially the observation and reconnaissance of defiles, choke points and possible obstacle crossing sectors."[50] They are broken down into 5 or 6 man teams. They are inserted by a variety of means (foot, vehicle, helicopter, water, or airborne) and are capable of operating out to 100 kilometers. Their mission is to locate high priority targets in the enemy division rear or corps forward support areas. Their primary mission is to report on the enemy and avoid engagements, but they have the "secondary mission to conduct disruptive operations in the enemy rear."[51]

This current organization and doctrine for human razvedka particularly the RAC is a product of Soviet experience. A large part of their experience is from the Great Patriotic War.

In June 1941, German forces poured into the Soviet Union. This offensive not only cost the Soviets millions of lives but also revealed an inept Soviet military still reeling from the leadership purges of the 1930's. Additionally, it exposed the total failure of Soviet intelligence. Not to be caught unprepared again, the Soviet military made broad and sweeping

32

changes to their entire force structure. The intelligence force structure was part of the momentum of change.

At the division, the Soviets created a reconnaissance company (see Diagram NO.9) for troop ground razvedka. Augmented with collection by other intelligence disciplines at all echelons of command, human razvedka helped build the mosaic of enemy capabilities and intentions.

Following this success at Stalingrad in November 1942, the Soviets continued to monitor German troop dispositions and attempt to clarify the picture of German operational intent. This intelligence collection brought the Soviet attention to Kursk, and by the spring of 1943 the Soviets anticipated a major German offensive in the area. The assault commenced in July 1943, and the Soviet assessment of German intentions was accurate. More important, Soviet human razvedka stayed active throughout the battle and kept track of German operational reserves within the depth of the German formations.

Although Soviet sources do not reveal the entire picture of Soviet doctrinal employment plans, depth of employment behind German lines, or communications means, open source Soviet material and previously classified documents reveal that intelligence obtained by "ground observation of rail and road routes was probably most important ... [and] the chief means for determining German intentions."[52] With their success at Kursk, the Soviets continued to reclaim the initiative and began a legacy of active Soviet tactical human intelligence collection.

The final push for the Soviets before their entrance into Berlin and the defeat of Hitler's Werhmacht was the Vistula-Oder operation in January 1945. In this operation, the Soviets were able to draw upon "over 3 years of war experience to employ imaginative intel techniques"[53] against a determined enemy. The Vistula-Oder operation was characterized by "bold and active"[54] _razvedka_ synchronized throughout the enemy depths for extended periods before and during the operation. Noteworthy of this operation and contributing to Soviet success was the practice of "employing long range intelligence reconnaissance detachments, often parachuted into the operational depths of the enemy rear."[55]

These elements operated for as long as two months from hidden bases well within the German rear area. The surveillance of Nazi units provided a measure of detail the Soviets had been previously unable to gather.

> Enemy artillery, 6 barrel mortars, and tank unit dispositions were discovered. Special attention was paid to the daily life of enemy forces and their daily routine. We knew when the fascist soldiers went to the field kitchen and when they left and when changes in security were made.[56]

34

Both operations reveal a Soviet force that had recovered from initial losses due in large part to an abject failure or total collapse of their intelligence collection doctrine and force structure. The result, however, was an improved, imaginative doctrine that actively sought intelligence and an associated improvement in the force design. They simultaneously improved their technical collection efforts by aviation and rudimentary communications intercept means but placed primary reliance on the "human factor as the most critical element ... always more important than technology."[57] The current Soviet doctrine reflects these lessons learned from the Great Patriotic War, and demonstrate the Soviet belief, acquired through experience that more tactical human razvedka is better. The US Army would be wise to examine the Soviet experience with LRS teams. We may not have the luxury of time or space to recover, as did the Soviets, from surprise and concomitant initial defeat. We must expect that the Soviets or their proxies, as potential adversaries, will rely on LRS type operations. We should be as prepared.

CHAPTER VI: CONCLUSIONS AND DOCTRINAL IMPLICATIONS

The division commander in a contingency corps operating in an immature theater and a forward deployed corps commander operating in a mature theater are expected, by doctrine, to perform at the same echelon of command. The significant similarity between these two echelons of command is the requirement to conduct deep operations, to shape the battlefield. However, the intelligence collection tools available to accomplish those similar missions are different.

A division commander operating in an immature theater cannot achieve the same depth with his own eyes and ears, yet he is told that he must. Much of what the corps commander has to accomplish his detect mission is not suited to contingency operations because of size, weight, set up time, or external support required when used in an austere or immature theater. The LRS assets do not share these deployability limitations. They are light weight, quickly deployable on almost any kind of troop transport aircraft, can be inserted with inherent but acceptable risks, and more important, are reliable and responsive to the commander.

Better than most available technical means for target detection, the LRS teams can develop the situation and specific targets for the commander. Intelligence collection continually feeds, in fact initiates, the deep targeting process. They have an all weather, day and night detection capability. They seldom need verification. They can provide accurate locational data down to 8 digits on a 1:50,000 scale map. They can conduct continuous operations.

Skeptics may concede the advantages of human

intelligence but will argue that technology, given the
time and the money, can create the genius collection
system to perform similarly with the same deployability
criteria but without the attendant risk associated with
of tactical human intelligence collection beyond the
shadow of the FLOT. There is no doubt that this is well
within the realm of possibility. The problem lies not
with the creativity of science but with the
availability of time and money. The plethora of threats
around the globe will not wait for the introduction of
a genius detection system nor does the army have the
money.

The challenge today for the division in a
contingency corps in an immature theater is to be able
to shape the deep battle, fight the close battle, and
do it with what he presently has. There is little
shaping of the deep battle that the division commander
can execute with his organic intelligence collection
assets. However, LRS teams can provide the deep-look
capability that the division commander needs but does
not have in sufficient quantity to make an impact on
his deep target detection mission. Corps has the assets
that division can use on a permanent basis.

LRS teams are a combat multiplier that can make a
greater impact at division than they can at corps in
contingency operations where a division is probably the
highest echelon of command in theater. LRS assets are

available today at no cost to the army -- no research
and development costs, no program start up costs, no
fielding costs.

There are several doctrinal implications
associated with the collection gap. First, doctrine is
the link between theory and practice. The current army
force structure for corps and division reflects the
theoretical differences between these two echelons of
command and their intended practice. Whether doctrine
stems from practice or from theory remains a conundrum;
however, doctrine does link theory and practice and
assumes many forms.

Doctrine covers how to fight and where to fight,
what weapons are available and when to use which
weapon, how to employ specific forces and how to
synchronize the efforts of many disparate units, what
size units to create and what specific military
occupational skills will best serve the organization.
The list goes on and on. Critical ingredients of
doctrine are how a unit is expected to fight, its
missions, and what a unit needs to accomplish its
required missions, its force structure.

Today's Army is expected to fight anywhere across
the spectrum of conflict from high to low-intensity
warfare. In fact, the Army has produced two field
manuals that explain the Army doctrine or, more
accurately, doctrines. The Army has not resolved

satisfactorily whether FM 100-5, Operations, and FM
100-20, Low Intensity Conflict, are two distict
doctrines or are variations of the parent field manual
100-1, The Army. Regardless, the Army is asking its
forces to fight across the spectrum of war, in both
mature and immature theaters, without adequately
equipping those forces earmarked principally for
contingency operations. The force structure for
divisions regardless of their mission focus reflects a
bias toward operations in a mature theater. The force
design for tactical human intelligence collection
assets in the division in a contingency corps ignores
its likely mission requirements. Doctrine does not
match practice.

The Army needs varied force structures to meet its
varied mission requirements. In particular, tactical
human intelligence in the division of the contingency
corps is inadequate. The Army needs to stop building
generic tools simply because they are appropriate for
the majority not necessarily the whole. The Army,
especially when cost is a factor and I'm not sure it
will ever not be a factor, must wisely allocate
resources to meet mission requirements. An 80 percent
solution is not good enough. The division of the
contingency corps must be able to meet its intelligence
collection mission requirements. Right now it can't.

The Achilles heel of the division in a contingency

corps is target detection. An increase in the organic LRS teams can help the division overcome its limitation. This collection gap must be and can be closed. It's time for the army to consider it and just do it.

DIAGRAM NO.1   STRUCTURE OF MODERN WARFARE AND ECHELONS
                OF COMMAND (FM 71-100)

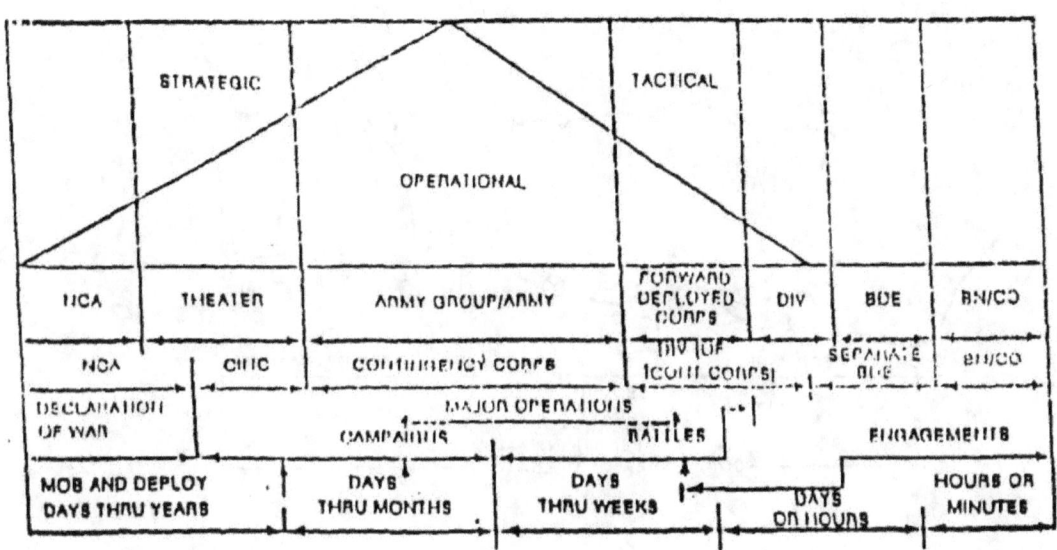

Extracted from FM 71-100 (<u>Division</u> <u>Operations</u>), p.1-2.

DIAGRAM NO.2 CORPS BATTLEFIELD STRUCTURE (FM 100-15)

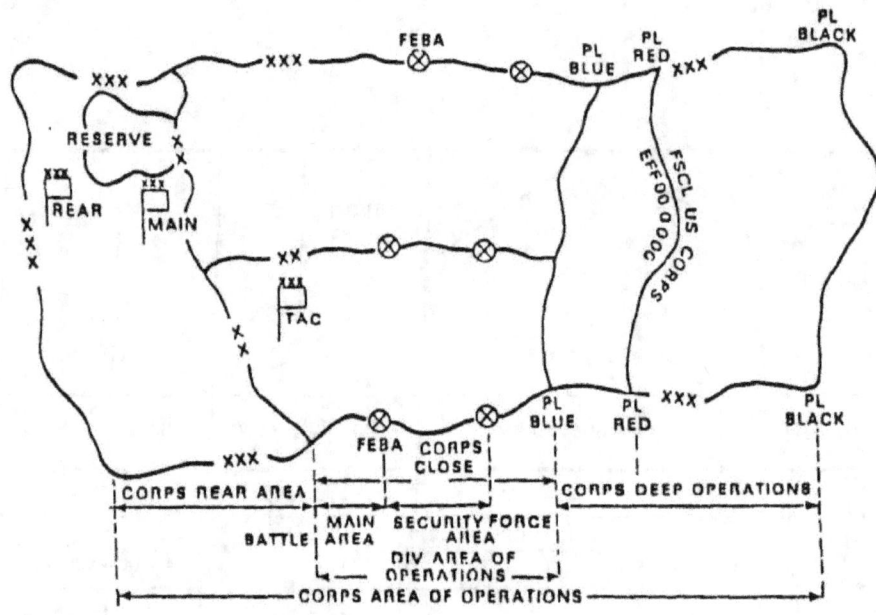

Extracted from FM 100-15 (Corps Operations), p.6-2.

DIAGRAM NO.3   CORPS INTELLIGENCE COLLECTION ASSETS IN THE
              MILITARY INTELLIGENCE BRIGADE (FM 34-1)

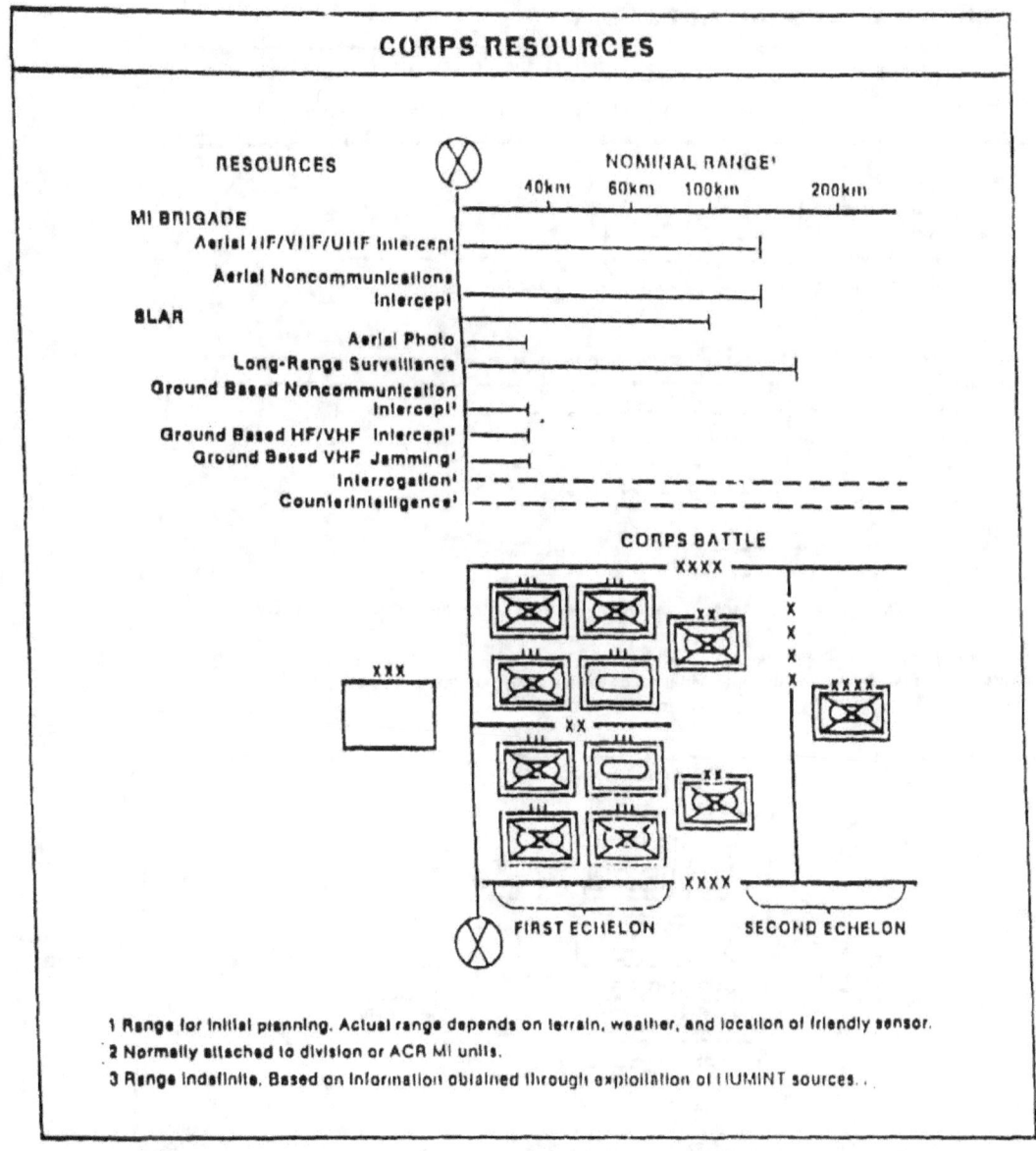

Extracted from FM 34-1 (Intelligence and Electronic Warfare
Operations), p.2-44.

DIAGRAM NO.4 DIVISION INTELLIGENCE COLLECTION ASSETS IN
THE MILITARY INTELLIGENCE BATTALION (FM 34-1)

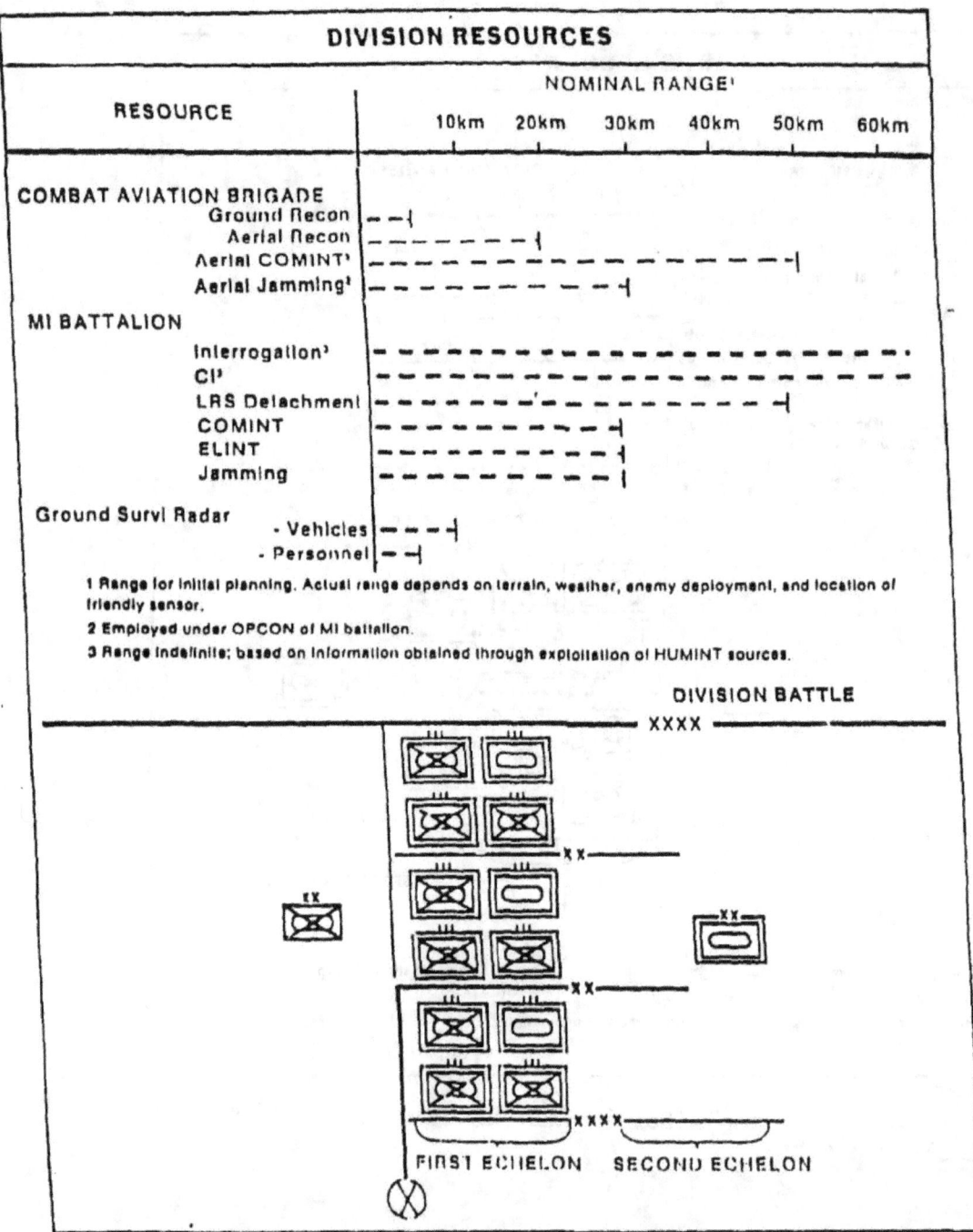

DIVISION RESOURCES

RESOURCE	NOMINAL RANGE[1]					
	10km	20km	30km	40km	50km	60km

COMBAT AVIATION BRIGADE
  Ground Recon
  Aerial Recon
  Aerial COMINT[2]
  Aerial Jamming[2]

MI BATTALION
  Interrogation[3]
  CI[3]
  LRS Detachment
  COMINT
  ELINT
  Jamming

Ground Survl Radar
  - Vehicles
  - Personnel

1 Range for initial planning. Actual range depends on terrain, weather, enemy deployment, and location of friendly sensor.

2 Employed under OPCON of MI battalion.

3 Range indefinite; based on information obtained through exploitation of HUMINT sources.

DIVISION BATTLE
XXXX

FIRST ECHELON   SECOND ECHELON

Extracted from FM 34-1 (Intelligence and Electronic Warfare
Operations), p.2-36,37.   44

DIAGRAM NO.5 SUPPORT ALLOCATION OF INTELLIGENCE COLLECTION
ASSETS FROM NEXT HIGHER ECHELON (FM 34-1)

IEW SYSTEM				
ECHELON	PRODUCERS	ORGANIC RESOURCES	ALLOCATED SUPPORT	REQUESTS SPT FROM
EAC	EACIC	MI Bde (EAC) Intgs S&T Intel HUMINT CI SIGINT HF ECM		USAF/USN/USMC National Allies
CORPS	CTOC SPT ELM	MI Bde Intg CI Spt Voice Coll (VHF) Aerial Noncom Intcp Aerial Comm Intcp VHF ECM (Grd) Noncom Intcp (Grd) SLAR, Photo IA Long-Range Survl	CI Spt Tech Intel Intgs	EAC USAF/USN/USMC National Allies
DIV¹ (HEAVY)	DTOC SPT ELM	MI Bn GSR Aerial Comm Intcp/DF/ECM (OPCON) CI Spt Voice Coll (VHF/HF/ECM) HF/VHF ECM Noncom Intcp/DF Intgs Long-Range Survl	Voice Coll (VHF) VHF ECM (Grd) Noncom Intcp (Grd) INT CI Spt	CORPS USAF
BDE	S2/BICC	No Resources²	IEW Spt Elm³ Survl Sqd IEW Co Tm C&J Plt CI Spt⁴ Intg⁴	Div
BN	S2/BICC	Scout Plt Troops Patrols	GSR Tms	BDE

NOTES:
1 ACR/separate brigade organic MI company provides support similar to divisional MI battalion adjusted to scale based on the mission.
2 Some resources are further allocated to the battalion.
3 IEW support element provides interface between MI assets and brigade S2/S3.
4 When corps augmentation is available.

Extracted from FM 34-1 (Intelligence and Electronic Warfare Operations), p.2-48.

DIAGRAM NO.6   EXAMPLE EMPLOYMENT OF CORPS AND DIVISION
LONG RANGE SURVEILLANCE TEAMS (FM 7-93)

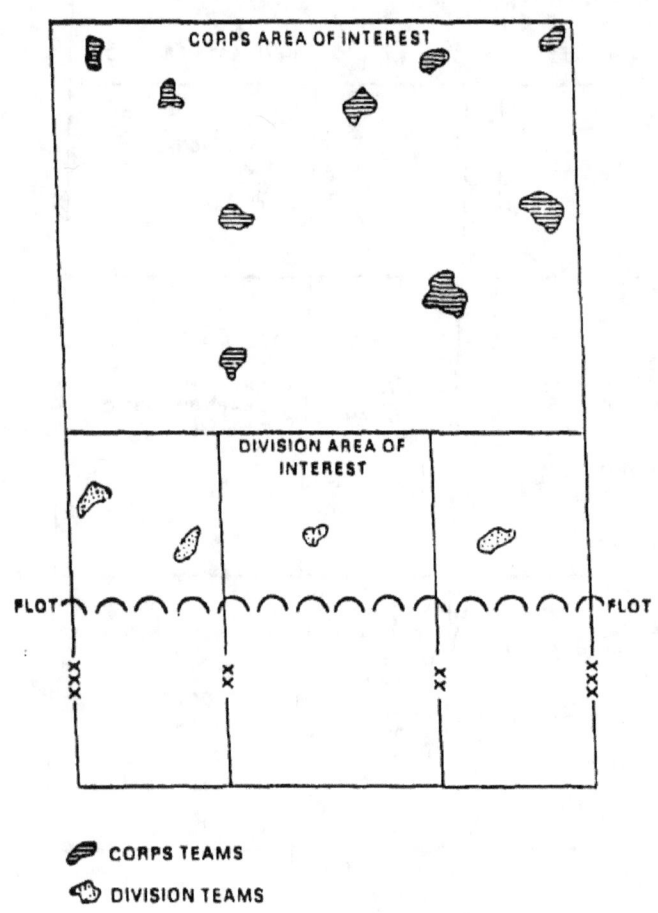

CORPS TEAMS

DIVISION TEAMS

Extracted from FM 7-93 (Long Range Surveillance Unit Operations),
p.2-8.

DIAGRAM NO.7   DEEP OPERATIONS - THE D3 METHODOLOGY ("CORPS
                DEEP OPERATIONS" dated SEPTEMBER 1989)

INTELLIGENCE SUPPORT TO
DECIDE, DETECT, DELIVER

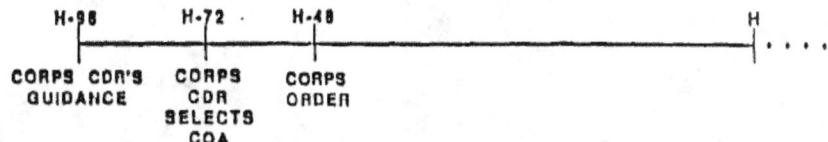

DECIDE

DETECT

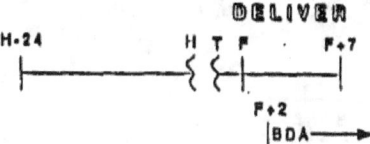

DELIVER

H - EXECUTION HOUR
T - TRIGGER EVENT
F - CROSS FLOT TIME FOR ENGAGEMENT SYSTEM

Extracted from Corps Deep Operations, pages not numbered.

DIAGRAM NO.8   DEEP OPERATIONS "SYSTEM OF SYSTEMS" ("CORPS
DEEP OPERATIONS" dated SEPTEMBER 1989)

UNCLAS. IED

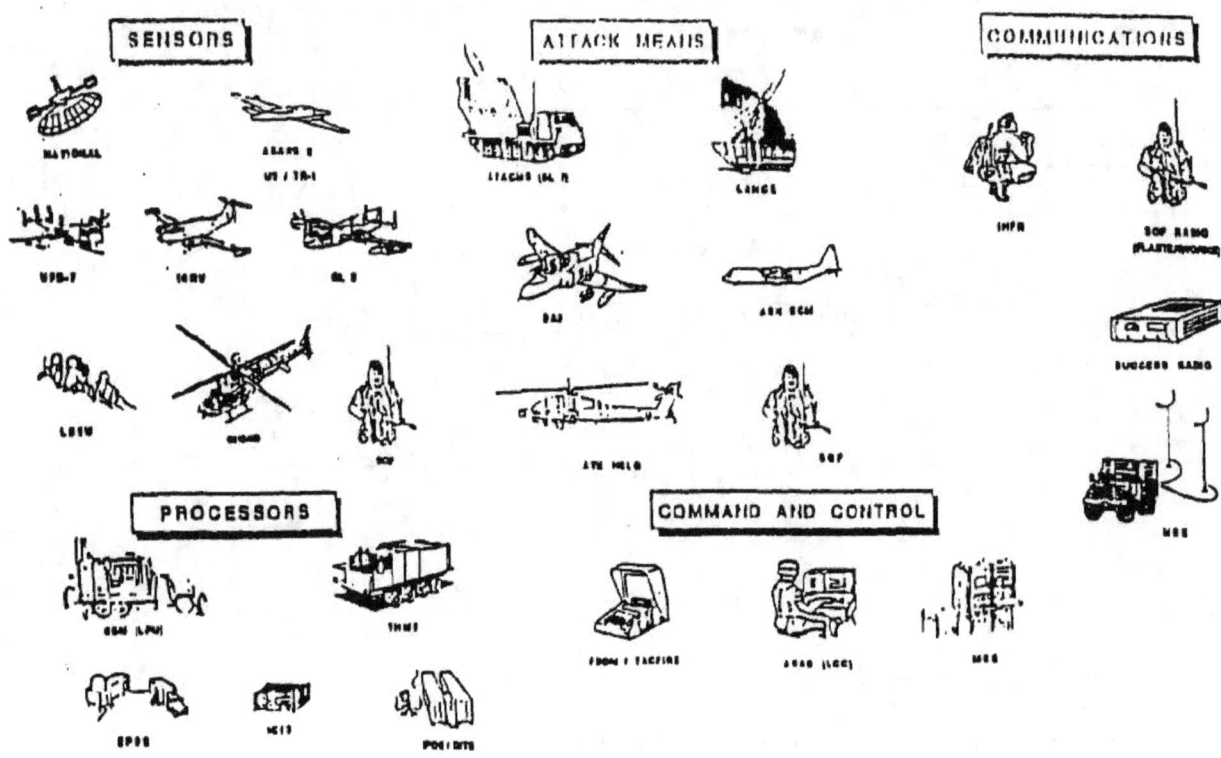

DEEP OPERATIONS SYSTEM OF SYSTEMS - 1990

UNCLASSIFIED

Extracted from Corps Deep Operations, pages not numbered.

DIAGRAM NO.9   INTELLIGENCE ORGANS OF DIVISION AND
REGIMENT (<u>SOVIET OPERATIONAL INTELLIGENCE IN
THE KURSK OPERATION</u>)

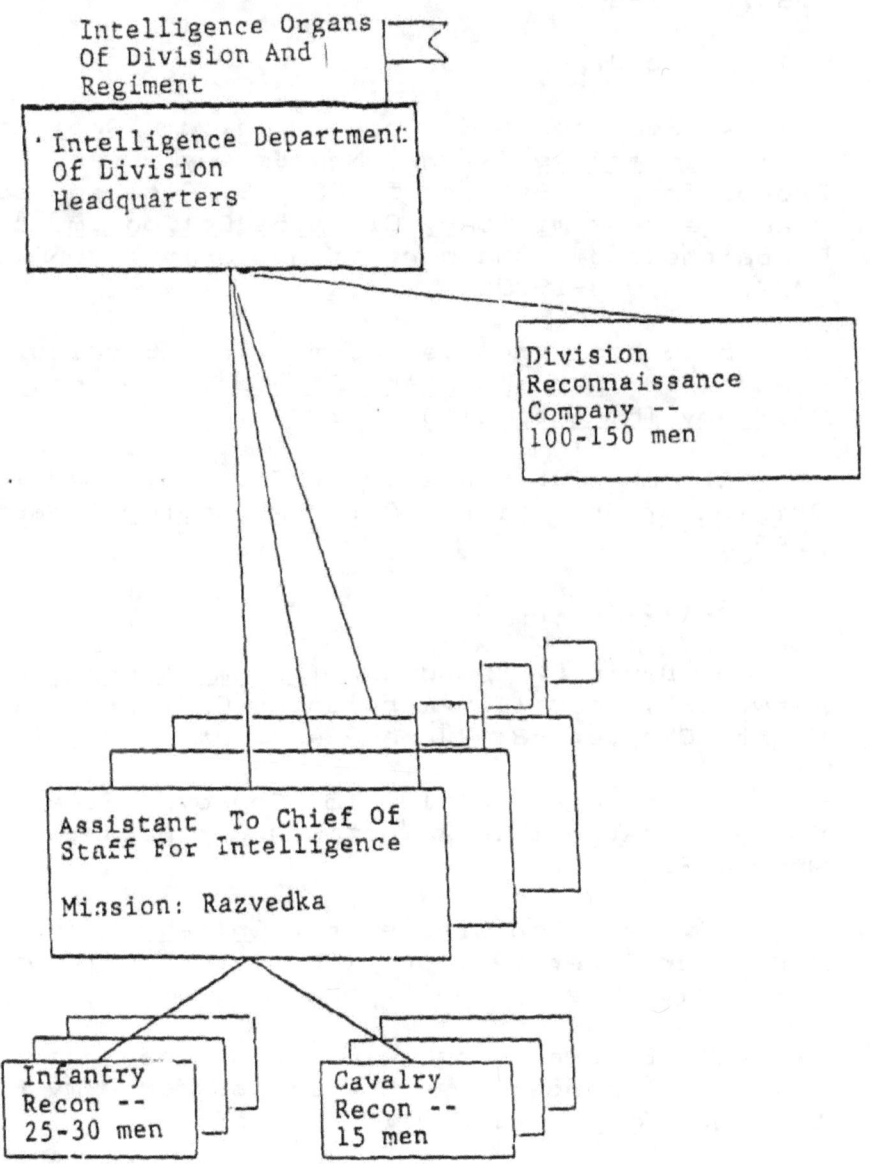

Intelligence Organs
Of Division And
Regiment

Intelligence Department
Of Division
Headquarters

Division
Reconnaissance
Company --
100-150 men

Assistant   To Chief Of
Staff For Intelligence

Mission: Razvedka

Infantry
Recon --
25-30 men

Cavalry
Recon --
15 men

Extracted from <u>Soviet Operational Intelligence in the
Kursk Operation</u>, p.13.

ENDNOTES

1. See discussions on "established theaters" and "developing theaters," Field Manual 100-15, Corps Operations (Washington D.C.: Department of the Army, 1989), p.1-2,3.

2. Field Manual 101-5-1, Operational Terms and Symbols (Washington D.C.: Department of the Army, 1985), p.1-60.

3. Ibid., p.1-68.

4. See Thomas E. Griess, editor, Ancient and Medieval Warfare (Wayne, New Jersey: Avery Publishing Group, Inc., 1984), pp.53-55, 59. Also see selected readings from Military Classics Colloquim, "The Classic Campaigns and Commanders of Antiquity," USACGSC course A037, AY 1988-1989.

5. School of Advanced Military Studies, Notes from class 1-08: War and Grand Strategy, Foundations of Military Thought, 11 July 1989.

6. James J. Schneider, "The Loose Marble and the Origins of Operational Art." Parameters, March 1989, p.89.

7. Ibid., p.88.

8. David G. Chandler, The Campaigns of Napoleon (New York: Macmillan Publishing Co., Inc., 1966), Part Eight, Chapter 42: "Jena-Auerstadt," pp.479-502.

9. Field Manual 100-15 (Approved Final Draft), Corps Operations (Washington D.C.: Department of the Army, 1988), p.1-2.

10. Carl von Clausewitz, On War, Michael Howard and Peter Paret, editors (Princeton: Princeton University Press, 1984), p.357.

11. General Crosbie E. Saint and Major Michael L. Hammack, "Changes Pose Challenges for Army Forces, Europe," Army, October 1988, p.56.

12. VII (US) Corps OPLAN, 1 April 1983, p.5.

13. V (US) Corps OPLAN, 7 March 1986, p.7.

14. Clausewitz, On War, p.358.

15. Ibid., p.357.

16. Ibid., p.524.

17. 82nd Airborne Division OPLAN, 6 June 1985, p. 2.

18. Ibid., p. 6.

19. Field Manual 71-100, Division Operations (Washington D.C.: Department of the Army, 1989), p. 1-6.

20. Ibid., p. 1-28.

21. FM 100-15 (AFD), p. 1-2.

22. Ibid., p. 1-4.

23. Ibid., p. 3-3.

24. FM 100-15, p. 6-2.

25. Field Manual 100-5, Operations (Washington D.C.: Department of the Army, 1986), p. 183.

26. Clausewitz, On War, p. 101.

27. Ibid., p. 102.

28. Ibid., p. 100.

29. Scott R. Gourley, "Tactical Intelligence is the Key to the AirLand Battle Scenario," Defense Electronics, February 1988, p. 44.

30. Field Manual 34-10, Division Intelligence and Electronic Warfare Operations (Washington D.C.: Department of the Army, 1986), p. 5-22.

31. James W. Rawles, "US Military Upgrades Its Battlefield Eyes and Ears," Defense Electronics, February 1988, p. 64.

32. Staff Sergeant David Schad, "Behind Enemy Lines," Soldiers, April 1988, p. 7.

33. Brigadier General David Henderson, The Art of Reconnaissance (London: John Murray, 1914), pp. 73-74.

34. Ibid., p. 74.

35. Ibid., p. 76.

36. The "Alamo Scouts" acquired their name from the Texas heritage of the Sixth Army commander, Lieutenant General Walter Krueger.

37. Major Billy E. Wells, Jr., "The Alamo Scouts: Lessons for LRSU's," Infantry, May 1989, p.27.

38. Ibid.

39. James W. England, Long Range Patrol Operations: Reconnaissance, Combat, and Special Operations (Boulder: Paladin Press, 1987), p.2.

40. Major General Joseph A. McChristian, The Role of Military Intelligence: 1965 - 1967 (Washington D.C.: Department of the Army, 1974), pp.104-105.

41. England, Long Range Patrol, p.4.

42. Ibid.

43. Field Manual 35-1, Intelligence and Electronic Warfare Operations (Washington D.C.: Department of the Army, 1984), p.3-31,32.

44. General Donn A. Starry, "Extending the Battlefield," Military Review, March 1981, p.32.

45. Field Manual 100-2-1, The Soviet Army: Operations and Tactics (Washington D.C.: Department of the Army, 1984), p.2-11.

46. Colonel David M. Glantz, The Fundamentals of Soviet Razvedka (Intelligence/Reconnaissance) (Fort Leavenworth: Soviet Army Studies Office, January 1989), p.68.

47. Ibid., p.69.

48. Ibid., p.67.

49. Tactical Commanders Development Course, Soviet Tactical Planning Factors (Fort Leavenworth: USACGSC, 1989), p.5-6.

50. Ibid., p.1-5.

51. Ibid., p.5-6.

52. Colonel David M. Glantz, Soviet Operational Intelligence in the Kursk Operation (July 1943) (Fort Leavenworth: Soviet Army Studies Office), p.51.

53. Colonel David M. Glantz, Soviet Operational Intelligence (Razvedka) in the Vistula - Oder Operation (January 1945) (Fort Leavenworth: Soviet Army Studies Office, undated), p.177.

54. Ibid., p.57.

55. Ibid., p.44.

56. Ibid., p.116.

57. Ibid., p.7.

BIBLIOGRAPHY

BOOKS

Chandler, David G. The Campaigns of Napoleon. New York:
    Macmillan Publishing Co., Inc., 1966.

Clausewitz, Carl von. On War. Edited and translated by
    Michael Howard and Peter Paret. Princeton:
    Princeton University Press, 1984.

England, James W. Long Range Patrol Operations:
    Reconnaissance, Combat, and Special Operations.
    Boulder: Paladin Press, 1987.

Glantz, David M. The Fundamentals of Soviet Razvedka
    (Intelligence/Reconnaissance). Fort Leavenworth:
    Soviet Army Studies Office, January 1989.

_____. Soviet Operational Intelligence in the
    Kursk Operation (July 1943). Fort Leavenworth:
    Soviet Army Studies Office, August 1988.

_____. Soviet Operational Intelligence
    (Razvedka) in the Vistula - Oder Operation
    (January 1945). Fort Leavenworth: Soviet Army
    Studies Office, undated.

Griese, Thomas E., editor. Ancient and Medieval
    Warfare. Wayne, New Jersey: Avery Publishing
    Group, Inc., 1984.

Henderson, Brigadier General David. The Art of
    Reconnaissance. London: John Murray, 1914.

Herbig, Katherine L. "Chance and Uncertainty in On
    War." In Clausewitz and Modern Strategy,
    pp. 95-116. Edited by Michael Howard. Totowa,
    NJ: Frank Cass and Company Limited, 1986.

McChristian, Major General Joseph A. The Role of
    Military Intelligence: 1965 - 1967. Washington
    D.C.: Department of the Army, 1974.

Modern Reconnaissance. Harrisburg: The Military Service
    Publishing Company, 1944.

Posen, Barry. The Sources of Military Doctrine. Ithaca:
    Cornell University Press, 1984.

Romjue, John L. From Active Defense to AirLand Battle:
    The Development of Army Doctrine 1973 - 1982. Fort
    Monroe: TRADOC, 1984.

Suvorov, Viktor. Spetsnaz: The Inside Story of Soviet Special Forces. New York: W.W. Norton and Co., 1988.

PERIODICALS

Gourley, Scott R. "Tactical Intelligence is the Key to the AirLand Battle Scenario." Defense Electronics, February 1988, pp.43-53.

Palastra, General Joseph T. "Biggest Command Gives Training Highest Priority." Army, October 1988, pp.44-54

Rawles, James W. "US Military Upgrades Its Battlefield Eyes and Ears." Defense Electronics, February 1988, pp.56-70.

Saint, General Crosbie and Hammack, Major Michael. "Changes Pose Challenges For Army Forces, Europe." Army, October 1988, pp.56-70.

Schad, Staff Sergeant David. "Behind Enemy Lines." Soldiers, April 1988, pp.6-9.

Schneider, James J. "The Loose Marble and the Origins of Operational Art." Parameters, March 1989, pp.85-99.

Starry, General Donn A. "Extending the Battlefield." Military Review, March 1981, pp.31-50.

Stillman, Captain Jeffery. "Soviet Reconnaissance, Part 1." Red Thrust, May 1989, pp.4-6.

Wells, Major Billy. "The Alamo Scouts: Lessons for LRSU's." Infantry, May - June 1989. pp.26-32.

GOVERNMENT PUBLICATIONS

Field Manual 7-93, Long Range Surveillance Unit Operations. Washington D.C.: Department of the Army, 1987.

_____ 34-1, Intelligence and Electronic Warfare Operations. Washington D.C.: Department of the Army, 1987.

_____ 34-10, Division Intelligence and Electronic Warfare Operations. Washington D.C.: Department of the Army, 1986.

_____ 34-25, Corps Intelligence and Electronic Warfare Operations. Washington D.C.: Department of the Army, 1987.

_____ 71-100, Division Operations. Washington D.C.: Department of the Army, 1989.

_____ 100-2-1, The Soviet Army: Operations and Tactics. Washington D.C.: Department of the Army, 1984.

_____ 100-5, Operations. Washington D.C.: Department of the Army, 1986.

_____ 100-15 (Approved Final Draft), Corps Operations. Washington D.C.: Department of the Army, 1988.

_____ 100-15, Corps Operations. Washington D.C.: Department of the Army, 1989.

_____ 101-5-1, Operational Terms and Symbols. Washington D.C.: Department of the Army, 1985.

National Training Center Memorandum for Lieutenant General Riscassi from Brigadier General Leland, Commander, NTC, 20 November 1985.

Tactical Commanders Development Course, Soviet Tactical Planning Factors. Fort Leavenworth: USACGSC, 1989.

OPLAN, 82nd Airborne Division, 6 June 1985.

OPLAN, V (US) Corps, 7 March 1986.

OPLAN, VII (US) Corps, 1 April 1983.

NOTES

School of Advanced Military Studies, Foundations of Military Theory. Notes From Class 1-08: War and Grand Strategy, 11 July 1989.

USACGSC Course A037, Military Classics Colloquim. Notes From Class MCC-2: "The Classic Campaigns and Commanders of Antiquity," AY 1988-1989.

www.ingramcontent.com/pod-product-compliance
Lightning Source LLC
Chambersburg PA
CBHW081421280526

45788CB00009B/3188